Out There?

MYSTERIOUS URBAN MYTHS

John Townsend

www.raintreepublishers.co.uk

Visit our website to find out more information about **Raintree** books.

To order:

☎ Phone 44 (0) 1865 888113

🖹 Send a fax to 44 (0) 1865 314091

💻 Visit the Raintree Bookshop at **www.raintreepublishers.co.uk** to browse our catalogue and order online.

First published in Great Britain by Raintree Publishers, Halley Court, Jordan Hill, Oxford OX2 8EJ, part of Harcourt Education Ltd. Raintree is a registered trademark of Harcourt Education Ltd.

Editorial: Charlotte Guillain and Isabel Thomas
Design: Michelle Lisseter and Bridge Creative Services Ltd
Picture Research: Maria Joannou and Kay Altwegg
Production: Jonathan Smith

Originated by Ambassador
Printed and bound in China and Hong Kong by South China

ISBN 1 844 43223 8
08 07 06 05 04
10 9 8 7 6 5 4 3 2 1

British Library Cataloguing in Publication Data
Townsend, John, 1924–
Mysterious urban myths. – (Out there)
1. Urban folklore – Juvenile literature
2. Curiosities and wonders – Juvenile literature
001.9'4

A full catalogue record for this book is available from the British Library.

Acknowledgements
Page 06, Corbis/Charles Gupton; 48, Corbis/; 04–05, Fortean Picture Library/; 05 bott, Photodisc; 05 mid, Corbis/Touhig Sion; 05 top, /Tudor Photography; 06–07, /Tudor Photography; 07, /Tudor Photography; 08, /Tudor Photography; 08–09, Topham Picturepoint/; 09, Photodisc/; 10, Stockbyte/; 10–11, Stockbyte/; 11, Corbis/Tim Page; 12, Corbis/Kim Sayer; 12–13, /Tudor Photography; 13, Alvey Towers/; 14–15, Corbis/Don Mason; 15, NHPA/Gerard Lacz; 16, Digital Vision/; 16–17, Ardea/Hans and Judy Beste; 17, Steve Bloom/; 18, NHPA/Trevor Mcdonald; 18–19, NHPA/Martin Harvey; 19, Corbis/Nik Wheeler; 20, NHPA/Gerard Lacz; 20–21, Photodisc/; 21, NHPA/Manfred Danegger; 22, Corbis/Ed Young; 22–23, Corbis/Phil Schermeister; 23, Corbis/ER Productions; 24, /Tudor Photography; 24–25, Corbis/Alan Goldsmith; 25, Ardea/A Weaving; 26–27, John Townsend, /Tudor Photography; 28, Corbis/Touhig Sion; 28–29, Rex Features/; 29, /Tudor Photography; 30, John Birdsall Photography; 30–31, /Tudor Photography; 31, /Tudor Photography; 33, /Tudor Photography; 36, Corbis Sygma/Curtis; 36, /Tudor Photography; 37, Snopes.com/; 38, /Tudor Photography; 39, Corbis/James A Sugar; 39, NHPA/Stephen Dalton; 40, Alamy Images/; 41, Hulton Archive and T Revelli; 41, Corbis/Steve Starr; 42, Alamy Images/; 42–43, /Tudor Photography; 43, Corbis/Bob Krist; 44, /Tudor Photography; 45, /Tudor Photography; 46, Corbis/Bob Krist; 46–47, Photodisc/; 47, NHPA/James Carmichael Jr; 48–49, /Tudor Photography; 49, Pictorial Press/; 50, Photodisc/; 26, Science Photo Library/Claude Nuridsany and Marie Perrennou.

Cover photograph reproduced with permission of Corbis/Thom Lang.

Every effort has been made to contact copyright holders of any material reproduced in this book. Any omissions will be rectified in subsequent printings if notice is given to the publishers.

CONTENTS

Any words appearing in the text in bold, **like this**, are explained in the Glossary. You can also look out for them in the Weird words box at the bottom of each page.

MYSTERIOUS TALES

TRUE OR FALSE?

The urban myths in this book are given a code:

(T) = TRUE
It is thought the story is based on real details.

(F) = FALSE
It seems the whole story is made up.

(?) = Who knows?
It is hard to tell how much of the story is made up.

Whether they are true or not, the stories are still worth telling.

Are urban myths just modern fairy tales for adults? **❯❯**

You can never tell. That is the mystery with **myths**. How much is really true? How much gets added each time the story is told?

WEIRD WORDS

absurd crazy or ridiculous
myth made-up tale, told over the years and handed on

THE MYSTERY OF URBAN MYTHS

Urban myths are told over and over again. Many were based on true events to begin with but often they are hard to believe. Many have mysterious endings. But the real mystery is in working out which stories have been made up.

ANY TIME, ANY PLACE

Urban myths are stories of our time. They could be told in any town around the world. They often begin with the words, 'You may not believe this but my friend's friend met someone who this really happened to…'

TELLING TALES

An urban myth is best when people believe it really happened to someone they know. Some urban myths have a message or a warning. Some have a spooky ring of truth. Many are funny and a few are scary. Most have more than a hint of the weird, **absurd** or the revolting. Mystery is never far away and there is often a twist at the end of the tale.

COMING SOON

New urban myths are being told all the time. Just where and how do they start? New tales of mystery are about to unfold…

FIND OUT LATER...

Just how mysterious was the note left on a car?

Should we believe the story of the killer cactus?

Can we explain what the dog had in its throat?

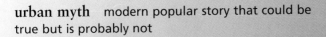

urban myth   modern popular story that could be true but is probably not

CRIME

Failed crooks make good stories, even though it is hard to tell if some people can really be so stupid…

THE CROOK WHO USED HER HEAD

On a hot day, a woman walked out of the supermarket and fainted. It must have been from the heat because she was wearing a fur coat and hat. A doctor ran over to cool her down, thinking she had heatstroke. He undid her thick coat and took off her hat. Now he could see what was wrong. Inside her coat was a frozen turkey and under her hat was a bag of frozen prawns. She was a shoplifter. She had chilled her blood, numbed her brain and got frostbite. (?)

You will never believe this, but I have just heard that a man in our street was arrested…

DID YOU KNOW?

- Urban myths are sometimes called urban **legends**.

- They are stories that people like to believe are true but they cannot be proved.

- People usually tell urban myths about a friend of a friend.

WEIRD WORDS   cashier   person who works on a till or at a bank
legend   story based on a grain of truth

HI-TECH LIE DETECTOR

The police had caught a robber but he would not admit to his crime. So the police tried a trick. They told him they were about to use a new **lie detector**. They got a pan from the kitchen and put it on his head. Wires went from the handle to the photocopier.

'Did you rob the store?' they asked.

'No,' he said.

The police pressed the copy button and paper came out of the photocopier. The word 'Lie' was printed on the paper. The robber gave up. 'Okay, you win. The machine knows the truth. I did it.'

The police got their man.

A nice story – but doubtful! ⑦

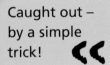

Caught out – by a simple trick! ❮❮

A crook with more than just a price on his head. ❯❯

SAME TRICK – STICKY END

Another story tells of a shoplifter with a bald head. He hid a frozen steak under his cap. By the time he got to the checkout it was thawing. Blood was dripping down his face. The **cashier** screamed. They took him to the emergency room and arrested him!

lie detector machine that records a person's reactions during questioning

CALL THE COPS!

Burglars broke into a house and one of them used the phone to call a friend. He was wearing gloves so he would not leave any fingerprints, but this made him press the wrong button. Instead of 998 he called 999. The police traced the call and arrested the crooks. Ⓣ

FOOLED

Even if all the details in these urban myths are not exactly true, the police deal with goings-on like this most weekends.

THE CHAINSAW MADMAN

A woman answered her door late one night and screamed at what she saw. She slammed the door and ran to phone the police. A man dressed in ski goggles and a hood stood on her doorstep, waving a roaring chainsaw. She hid upstairs, fearing she was about to be the next victim of the chainsaw-madman.

Police raced to her house but when they arrived the chainsaw-madman had gone. The woman was a nervous wreck. Police began to search the area.

Dialing with gloves on was a bad idea for the crook who called the police by mistake! ❮❮

WEIRD WORDS   awkward   shy and foolish
intruder   burglar who breaks in to someone's property

WRONG ADDRESS

Police found the **sinister** figure at the door of another house. They grabbed him at gunpoint, threw his chainsaw to the ground and stretched him out on the lawn. The front door opened and inside there was a fancy dress party in full swing. The man the police had arrested was a guest. He had dressed up as the hell-raising rap star Eminem and wanted to burst into the party with style.

The police said later, 'It turned out that the man had called at the wrong door earlier. He scared the woman out of her wits so he ran off feeling very **awkward**.' **?**

This costume was too realistic!

IT COULD HAPPEN...

In 1992, a 16-year-old student from Japan was in Louisiana in the USA. The student was asked to a Halloween party. He did not know the area and rang the wrong doorbell, wearing his scary costume. He was shot dead when the house owner mistook him for an **intruder**. **T**

sinister   harmful or evil

SURPRISE, SURPRISE

A woman found a dead cat by her parked car. She decided to take it home and bury it so she put it in her shopping bag. Just then a thief came by on a motorbike and snatched the bag. When he looked inside, he swerved off the road and crashed. (?)

KEEPING A CLOSE WATCH

Peter had just got on the train when he saw that his watch was missing. As the train began to move, he turned to see a boy on the platform who was waving and tapping his wrist, saying 'Just in time'. Thinking the boy had stolen his watch, Peter reached out of the train and grabbed the boy's collar, only to rip it off as the train moved away. He called his wife on his mobile to tell her what had happened. Before he could speak, she said, 'I've been trying to get hold of you. Did you know you left your watch behind on the table this morning?' (?)

leathers   clothes for wearing on a motorbike

HOLD UP

A delivery boy was paid by a friend to take a message and a bag to the bank. He sped off on his motorbike, parked outside the bank, went inside and handed the envelope to the **cashier**, as he had been told. All of a sudden the alarms went off. Guards rushed around him as he stood calmly in his **leathers** and crash helmet. The guards pointed guns at his head. 'Freeze!'

Later at the police station, they showed him the note that was inside the envelope.

> Fill the bag with money. I've got a gun. I'm not afraid to use it. No funny stuff.

The only funny stuff was his friend's idea of a joke.

Better than a night on the street?

Not every bag is what it seems...

COMMON MYTHS ABOUT THE POLICE

- The police cannot arrest you for speeding if they cannot keep up with you.
- If you know the secret word, you just whisper it to the police and they will let you off.
- Tramps always try to get arrested so they can have a warm bed for the night.

All Ⓕ

THE MESSAGE

The owner of a smart sports car kept alarms, chains, locks and clamps on his car to make sure it was safe. Now he could sleep at night. One morning his car was still chained but it had been turned around. A note under the wiper blade read: 'If we want this car, we'll take it.' ⓕ

CAR TROUBLE

Cars are in many urban myths. These **tall stories** about cars and their owners tell of events on the wrong side of the law.

TAKEN FOR A RIDE

A family lived in the rich part of town. One of their cars on the drive was a sports car. They always left the keys inside this car. One morning it was missing and no one knew where it was. A few hours later the car was back in the drive with a note. It said:

Dear Neighbours, please forgive us. We live nearby and had a family emergency.

We had to borrow your car without asking. Please accept these tickets as thanks.

No car is safe from a determined thief.

culprit   guilty person

A KIND THOUGHT

Tickets for all the family to the theatre the next week were pinned to the note.

'How kind,' they thought. 'What friendly neighbours. They've even cleaned the car for us.'

Next week they all went to the theatre with their free tickets. When they returned home, they found another note on the front door. It said: "Hope you enjoyed the show. We missed the sports car!"

As the family went indoors, they found the lights did not work. There were no light bulbs. In fact, the whole house was empty. They looked around in horror in the dark. Everything they owned had been stolen. **F**

GOOD NEWS AND BAD NEWS

A woman came back to her parked car and found it had been dented. Then she saw a note on the windscreen and thought the **culprit** had left his details.

I've just bashed your car. A crowd is watching me. Good news: I'm writing this to look as if I'm leaving my name. Bad news: I'm not!

? It seems likely that the dented car story has happened. **‹‹**

ANIMALS

AN OLD STORY WITH MANY TWISTS

The sick dog myth goes back at least 60 years.

- Sometimes the pet is a cat.
- Sometimes the food is salmon, mushrooms or cold meat.
- Sometimes the pet has been killed by a car.

But the poor guests always end up at the hospital!

Poisoned, bashed on the head or playing dead?

Urban myths about pets are often funny because we never quite understand animals.

THE SICK DOG

A woman was preparing for an important dinner party. Her husband's new boss was coming so she spent all morning cooking fresh prawns. The dog ate one so she put him outside just as the guests arrived. After they had eaten the prawns, a neighbour called and said, 'Your dog looks very ill'. The woman was afraid that the prawns had poisoned the dog so she took all the guests to hospital to get their stomachs pumped. When she got home another neighbour asked, 'Is your dog all right? I'm afraid I dropped a brick on his head.' (?)

WEIRD WORDS horrified shocked and disgusted

WHOSE DOG?

A girl wanted to get on the right side of her old rich aunt. They had not met for years so the girl called round. As she was ringing the doorbell, a little dog came yapping at her feet. It followed her into the large house. The girl talked with her aunt in a very smart room, with the dog jumping on the fine furniture, sniffing the cakes and running mud over the carpet. The girl thought what a nasty dog it was but she thought she had better be kind about it. 'What a lovely little dog you have, auntie.'

Her aunt looked **horrified**. 'I thought the horrible thing was yours!' ⓘ

ANIMAL MYTHS

- A swan will break your leg with its wing if you get near.
- Bats like to tangle in your hair.
- If you hold a dog's lower jaw, it cannot bite you.
  Ⓕ – most of the time!

A popular animal myth is that parrots find swear words easier to learn. Perhaps it depends on their owner! ❬❬

15

CAN YOU BELIEVE IT?

RHINO RUMP

A superglue salesman was showing a party of Russian customers round his city. He took them to the safari park and said. 'Our superglue is so strong I could stick my hands to that rhino.'

The man put a few drops on his hands and placed them on the rhino's rear end. They stuck tight but the rhino did not like it. It ran round its pen, with the salesman dragging behind. The angry rhino had to be drugged before the man's hands could be released.

The Russians bought three crates of the glue. **F**

Some people will go to any lengths to sell something.

What has this snake eaten to cause such a large bulge?

Rhinoceros is not just the name given to a large, thick-skinned animal with a horn. There is also a rhinoceros beetle. For its size, this beetle is one of the world's strongest animals. It can carry 850 times its own weight. That is like a person being able to carry ten elephants. **T**

16   **WEIRD WORDS**   paddy field   flooded field where rice is grown

SWALLOWED BY A SNAKE

Three boys were recently camping in the jungle in South America. In the middle of the night one boy woke up to feel something sliding over his leg. He sat up to tell the others but only one friend was there. They shone a torch outside the tent, only to see a huge snake moving away from the tent. It was so fat it could hardly move. They grabbed hold of it and managed to cut it open. Their friend was inside and still alive. Ⓕ

This particular myth is not true but it could happen. A giant boa constrictor can swallow a deer whole. A boy would be a snake snack.

A boa squeezes its prey to death before swallowing it whole.

SNAPPY SALTIE

A tourist in Northern Australia wanted to take a photo of a saltwater crocodile at a lake. He took a snap – but the croc took a snap back. It bit off his arm. When the lab developed his photo, two workers fainted and one was sick. Ⓕ

Imagine finding this beast in your bathroom … ▶▶

THE SEWERS OF NEW YORK

Our fear of large **reptiles** has brought about many urban myths about teeth. For years people have told stories of huge alligators living in the drains of large cities. They grow fat on sewer rats and all the waste.

WHERE DO THEY COME FROM?

There is a big **trade** in baby alligators. People think they are cute pets to keep in fish tanks. But the alligators grow too big. In the end people flush them away. Down they go to make a nest below the city. Then they breed down there. Some sewer workers have gone down to repair drains and have never been seen again… Ⓕ

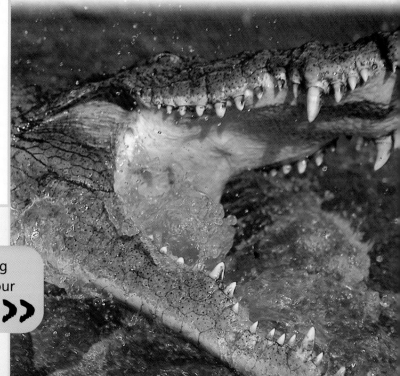

reptile   group of cold-blooded animals
thrive   to grow with strength and health

CROCODILE TEARS?

A young man moved into a basement apartment in New York. One night he was sitting on the toilet when he felt a terrible pain in his left buttock. He leapt up to find a small alligator hanging from his behind. The animal had squeezed up through the drains in its search for fresh meat.

When the man went to the hospital to have stitches, the doctor said this was now a common injury. Alligator teeth often chew human behinds!

NO NEED TO WORRY

Alligators **thrive** in sunny Florida. But it is hard to believe they could survive in the New York sewer system where the winters can be very cold.

GOLFING HANDICAP

On a golf course at Palm Beach in Florida, USA, an alligator lay in wait in a pond by the fifth green. A golfer went ahead from his friends to find his ball – and was never seen again. The police supposedly opened up the alligator and found the golfer inside.

Some golf courses are more challenging than others.

EXPERTS SAY...

Eagles do not normally swoop down and carry off small dogs. Some may attack a dog on the ground, and some may even briefly lift one up in the air, but it is rare for an eagle to make off with a dog. Then again, it is possible.

Another reason to keep small dogs on leads. ❖❖

BIRD ATTACKS

Myths about bird attacks are **far-fetched** – but some eagles are very big. Perhaps now and again there could be truth in some **rumours**…

VALDEZ, ALASKA

A woman in Alaska screamed as a bald eagle flew down and snatched her small dog up into the air. The pet was in the front garden when the eagle swooped down from a nearby tree. Before the woman could act, the eagle was off, gripping the yapping dog in its claws. **(?)**

MAINE, USA

A great horned owl was once said to have taken off with a 10 kilogram **Pekinese** dog.
It then went after a cat and an old woman. This myth has yet to be proved. **(F)**

far-fetched   sounds too strange to be true
Pekinese   breed of small dog with long hair

FLYING HIGH

In 1932, a four-year-old was playing out in the yard of her home in Leka in the north of Norway. Suddenly a huge sea eagle dived out of the sky. Its wingspan was 2.5 metres. Its **talons** dug into her arms as it rose up in the air and flew up to a cliff a mile away. Finally the eagle dropped the girl on a ledge. She screamed and her parents found her. She was fine. They kept her dress with the holes from the talons as proof. Her name is Svanhild Hansen. Hard to believe, but this story is true. (T)

UP, UP AND AWAY

If eagle owls can carry off big rabbits, small dogs could easily be on the menu. In February 2000, a small dog was scooped up by an eagle owl in the UK. The dog escaped and got back home. He was scratched, but he got over his first flight. (T)

Beware: eagle owls are stronger than they look. »

rumour   story based on gossip
talons   claws of a bird of prey

21

MEDICAL MYTHS

Hospitals are full of weird stories. Amongst the pain, there is often a funny side. Medical myths can certainly make us smile.

THE FARMER'S HAND

A farmer had an accident in his combine harvester and cut off his hand. He picked up the hand, drove to the local shop and packed it in frozen peas. Later he parked the combine harvester at **A&E** and got doctors to sew his hand back on.

There are real reports similar to this. (?)

Rachel will never forget her summer job! 〉〉

NURSING HOME

Rachel was glad to get a holiday job in the summer. It was in a nursing home. One old lady said she felt ill and as night fell, she got worse. They sent for the doctor. The priest came and gave the **last rites**, just in time. It was too late for the doctor now.

It was Rachel's job to lay out the body. She washed the old lady and got her ready for the **undertaker**. She brushed her hair and folded her hands over her chest.

A&E   accident and emergency department in a hospital
last respects   final farewell to someone who has died

LAST RESPECTS

The old lady's family came to pay their **last respects**. They all sat round the bed in silence. The only sound was the slow ticking of the clock. Suddenly there was a noise and someone screamed.

HAPPY ENDING

Everyone looked up. The old lady sat up with a smile. 'Ooh, I'd love a cup of tea,' she said. They could not believe it.

The strange thing was, the old lady had done the very same thing the year before. All her family could do was tear up the plans they had made for the funeral and put the kettle on! (T)

Could this really happen? You bet. It was Rachel herself who told this story.

THE FALSE LEG

Two thugs came across an old man who was limping. One thug kicked him and the old man's false leg flew up in the air. The leg fell back to earth, kicking the thug in the mouth and knocking him flat.

It is a good story but, like the leg, it is false. (F)

Would the evidence stand up in court? 〉〉

TRAVEL BUG

A student went backpacking around the world for her **gap year**. When she came back, she found a red mark on her hand. She put cream on it but her skin was really itchy. One day she gave it a hard scratch. The skin burst and out popped hundreds of baby spiders. Ⓕ

NASTY INSIDES

There is nothing more revolting than the thought of living things getting inside our bodies. Urban myths **thrive** on such **grisly** ideas.

SPROUTS

A schoolboy in the UK had a close shave. One evening his mother told him to wipe his nose as he had something green poking out of one nostril. He could not get rid of it, so his mother took a closer look and saw a small leaf sticking out of his nose. She gave it a tug and began to pull out a tomato plant. It was growing inside his nose. It was firmly attached and just would not come out.

Another good reason not to scratch spots.

gap year   break between school and further education

BRAIN FOOD

A few months before, the boy had sneezed while eating a tomato. One of the tomato seeds must have shot up his nose and got stuck. And that is where it began to sprout, where it was dark, warm and wet.

The boy was rushed to hospital where doctors had to operate. It was a very close thing. In just a few more days, the roots would have damaged his brain. They removed the plant whole, put it in a little pot and let him take it home to grow in the greenhouse.

This is a well-known myth. It is a great tale but utter nonsense. 🅕

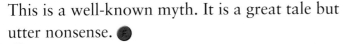

BAD HAIR DAY

A schoolgirl had very long hair. She kept it piled up on her head and did not wash it. In a maths lesson there was a clicking noise and her hair started moving. At first it seemed to be lice. But the school nurse found a nest in her hair – alive with cockroaches. 🅕

---

grisly   causing horror and disgust

ONE IN THE EYE

Before a woman got on the plane home from Africa, she got dust in her eye. During the flight, her eye got so sore she needed medical help when she got to the airport. Imagine her horror when the doctor removed a freshly hatched maggot from under her eyelid. **F**

Perhaps the cleaners are the most dangerous thing in a hospital! **»**

SWITCHED OFF

One hospital had a real mystery. On Fridays there were always more deaths in one of the wards. The mystery was only solved after a few months. A doctor just happened to be walking past when a cleaner was at work. She polished the floor in the 'intensive care' ward each Friday. The doctor watched in horror as she went to the socket on the wall to plug in her floor polisher. She pulled out the plug that was already in the socket – and unplugged three patients' life-support systems!

This story has become a bit of a classic. But do not worry – it is totally untrue. We hope. **F**

defrost   remove frost or ice from something
embarrass   make someone feel awkward and ashamed

STUCK

Doctors tell many stories about people who get stuck in **embarrassing** places.

One winter a woman got her lips stuck to her car door. She could not call for help and waited hours for someone to get a doctor. She had tried to **defrost** the lock by blowing on it. Her lips had frozen to the metal door. ⑦

STUCK FAST

A man got stuck in a toilet seat in a train. As the train gained speed, it sucked him down even tighter. When the train shot into a tunnel the **suction** suddenly reversed. He shot off the seat and his head got stuck in the towel holder. Doctors had to free him. ⑤

MEDICAL BLUNDERS

- In Wales a patient fell ill after a daffodil somehow got into the hospital dinner.
- In Holland a student doctor was sacked after roaring through the ward on a motorbike.
- A patient's behind caught fire when equipment set light to **surgical spirit** on the operating table.

  ⓣ All

> Hospital food can be really strange. ❮❮

suction   *gripping by sucking out air*
surgical spirit   flammable fluid used for keeping things clean

SCARY TALES

STILL ALIVE

A woman went to the butcher to get some cheap meat for her dog. The butcher found her a cow's heart. When she got home, she unwrapped the meat to put on a plate but it moved. The heart was beating and it jumped from her hands. 🅔

People have always loved stories that send shivers down their back. Urban myths have their fair share of tales to scare.

OUT IN THE BUSH

A woman was driving home late one night in her four-wheel drive jeep. It was a **remote** road in the **outback** in Australia, where robbers often struck. Ahead of her she saw a car parked across the middle of the narrow road. It was not wise to slow down so she pushed her foot down on the accelerator pedal. She roared off the road and over the bumpy **scrub**. The jeep bumped along then turned back on to the road past the car.

ambush   to lie in wait to attack
outback   Australia's wild country, miles from the towns

THE NEXT DAY

When the woman got home, she phoned the police to tell them about the mysterious vehicle.

The chilling evidence of an unwanted passenger... **>>**

In the morning, the police asked for more information. She told them how she had driven her jeep at high speed off the road, through the scrub, and then back on to the road.

The police told her she had been very lucky. She had driven over and killed the three armed men who were lying in wait to **ambush** her. They had been killers with a price on their heads. Now all they had were tyre marks on their heads.

Maybe most people want this myth to be true. Sadly it is just made up! (F)

Driving along a deadly quiet road is enough to scare anyone. **<<**

THE PASSENGER

A woman was driving along a lane late one night. A car behind flashed its lights, overtook her and pulled up. The driver ran towards the woman's car just as someone jumped out of her back door. 'Did you know,' the man said, 'there was someone on your back seat with an axe?' (F)

---

remote far-away place in the middle of nowhere
scrub thorny bushes and tufts of grass

MYSTERY MYTHS

Many scary urban myths have the same ideas.

- A dangerous **intruder** has broken in.
- He is still in the room or somewhere in the house.
- One female is unaware of what **lurks** just a few metres away.

These scary myths are often told late at night. Even though they are not true, **nervous** people may feel a shudder...

LATE NIGHT STUDENT

Two girls shared a room at college. One was studying late in the library and went back to their room to get her notes. She left the light off so she would not **disturb** her roommate. She felt around the desk, got her papers and left. Much later she went back to the room and this time she turned on the light. Her roommate was dead. She had been killed. There was writing in lipstick on the mirror: 'Aren't you glad you didn't turn on the light?'

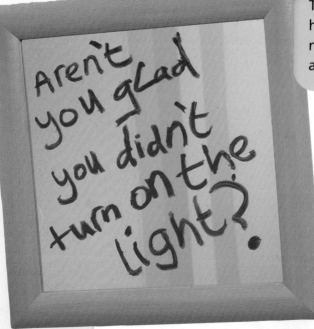

This creepy message has made the late night student myth a favourite. ««

disturb break someone's rest
lurk to wait around, ready to strike

THE BABYSITTER

A girl was babysitting late at night in an old **rambling** house. She was alone in charge of a sleeping baby. The phone rang so she picked it up. There was a scary voice on the other end that told her she was going to be strangled. The calls came every five minutes. She felt very scared and reported the calls to the phone company. Then the phone rang again. This time it was the telephone operator. The news was chilling. 'Get out quickly. Those calls are coming from the other phone in the house.'

But we should not be too scared. It is just a myth – we think. ⓔ

The dog in this myth is always a Rottweiler. ᐱᐱ

The story of a babysitter getting scary phone calls has been used in horror movies. ⌄⌄

AN OLD FAVOURITE

A woman arrived home to find her dog choking. She took the dog to the vet and left it overnight. Later the vet phoned in panic. He told her to get out of the house quickly. Human fingers were stuck in the dog's throat. The injured intruder could still be in the house. ⓠ

nervous   easily scared
rambling   lots of parts all over the place

NEARLY DEAD

Myths like this are well known – but they are just right for telling in the dark.

A woman was at a bar on her own when a stranger began to chat to her. They both got on well and she did not notice when he slipped powder into her drink.

THE NEXT MORNING

The woman opened her eyes. She was freezing and felt a pain in her back. She was lying in a bath in a hotel room and the bath was full of ice. As she sat up, she saw the note. It said:

SCARY HAND

Bus drivers find all sorts of things left behind on the seats in their buses. People do not just leave behind shopping or gloves. Not long ago a driver found a plastic bag on his bus. When he looked inside the bag he saw a human hand. ⑦

I have taken out one of your kidneys. Call 999 straight away but do not get out of the bath. ⑦

The driver in this myth got a nasty surprise! ➤➤

cleaver   knife with a heavy, wide blade

THE HITCHHIKER

A man was driving along a country road late at night. Suddenly he saw a girl hitchhiker in his lights so he stopped the car. 'You'd better get in,' he said. 'It's a cold night to be out walking.' She smiled and got into the car.

Soon they came to a village. 'I live here,' she said, pointing to a house. The man stopped the car and let her out but she just vanished. He went to the house to see if she had gone inside. A woman opened the door and said his mysterious passenger was her daughter who had died on the road that very night the year before. Ⓕ

HAIRY HAND

A man stopped his car to give an old woman a lift. After a few miles, the old woman's coat and scarf slipped. The driver saw a hairy hand gripping a handbag, with a meat **cleaver** sticking out of it. It was covered in fresh blood. Ⓕ

Never trust an old lady with a hairy hand... ❯❯

MISTAKES

WHEN THINGS GO WRONG

Why are many urban myths funny?

Maybe it is because they could happen to any of us.
People are:

■ just unlucky,
■ plain stupid,
■ caught out.

We can laugh because we do not know the people involved or if the events really happened.

There is nothing like other people's blunders to make good urban myths.

OOPS

A man and his wife decided to go to the shops in their car. But the car would not start. 'I'll stay and fix it. You go on the bus,' the man said.

When his wife came home, the car was still in the drive. Legs were sticking out underneath. She gave one leg a quick squeeze and said, 'Hi, sweetie'. But when she went indoors, her husband was in the kitchen. They rushed outside to find the man from the local garage still lying under the car. He had knocked himself out when he bashed his head in surprise. ⑦

It is hard to tell a person by their legs. And embarrassing if you get it wrong. ❯❯

OOPS AGAIN!

Two students went on holiday and decided to stay an extra day. It meant they missed a maths exam. They were not worried because they planned to tell the **professor** they were late back due to a flat tyre. How could he possibly know they were lying?

TOUGH QUESTION

When the students got back to college they told the professor their story and asked if they could sit the exam another time. He agreed but said that they had to sit the exam in separate rooms. They did this and both found the exam very easy. But then they read the last question, worth 95 per cent of the total marks. It was a very short question with only four words: 'Which tyre was flat?' ⑦

UNHAPPY CAT

Many new urban myths spread quickly on the Internet. A **fake** photo can make them seem real. A woman took her cat to have its fur trimmed. She asked for a line cut, which is just a trim. They thought she said 'a lion cut'. ⑦

Some people give their pets the strangest haircuts. ❯❯

professor   teacher in a university

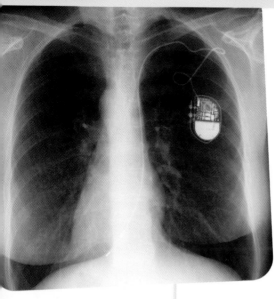

HI-TECH GAFFS

Whether it is mobile phones cooking your brain cells or the television remote control setting off the neighbour's car alarm – we live in an age where gadgets can go wrong. Modern **technology** is behind many urban myths.

MICROWAVE TROUBLE

A busy hotel kitchen fitted a new top-of-the-range microwave oven. There was just the place for it in the kitchen on a low shelf at waist height. The chef was pleased with his new gadget. He could reheat many dishes in it at the same time. It was extra large and had a 'super-strength' button. The first time he used this button was also his last.

GADGET MYTHS

- **Pacemakers** can cause heart attacks going through airport security screens.
- A new virus attacks all computers every Friday 13th unless you have special software.
- Mobile phones can cause forest fires in Australia and explosions on oil rigs.

Believe these and you will believe anything. Ⓕ

Chef's special tonight – kidney surprise!

pacemaker   electronic device for helping to steady the heart beat

COOKED TO A SIZZLE

A customer asked for a steak and kidney pie – piping hot and well done. This was just the job for the new microwave on 'super-strength'. The chef pressed the button and turned his back on the microwave. As he beat some eggs, he was shocked to see them steam and bubble. But so did his insides, just before he fell dead on the floor.

The microwave door did not seal properly. All the microwaves leaked out. They not only cooked the kidneys in the pie but they cooked the chef's kidneys to a frazzle.

A true story? No, it is false. Even so, some people never trust microwave ovens. **F**

INTERNET TOILETS

There was a **rumour** on the Internet that Microsoft had invented the iLoo. It was a portable toilet where people could also use the Internet. A businessman was supposedly using one at Dallas Airport when the computer crashed. He was stuck inside the room for six hours. **F**

FW: 'Check out this new toilet!'

AERIAL FOR BROADBAND INTERNET CONNECTION

COMPUTER PLASMA SCREEN

WATERPROOF COMPUTER KEYBOARD

FLAT SCREEN SWIVELS OUT

WIRELESS KEYBOARD CAN BE USED ON LAP

COMPUTER WITH 6 CHANNEL SURROUND SOUND

Don't believe everything you read on the Internet. **◄◄**

DEAD ENDS

DEATH BY POTATO

A boy jammed a potato up the exhaust pipe of his teacher's car. He waited in the bushes to watch the car explode. The teacher drove off – but the hot potato shot out and hit the boy smack between the eyes. **F**

People who pass on urban myths like to tell stories about **villains** who come to a sticky end. If someone in an urban myth gets what he or she deserves, it seems we can smile, however horrible the ending is. **Bizarre** deaths are only interesting when we are not involved!

THE CURSE OF THE CAR

A man called Jones bought his dream car on 17 October 1989. It was a fancy red Porsche. He drove off to watch a baseball game in California in the USA. During that historic game, an earthquake hit the city of San Francisco. The game was called off as people ran for their lives.

be careful when you play a practical joke – it could backfire!

WEIRD WORDS   bizarre   very strange or weird

SHOCK HORROR

Jones ran from the stadium with everyone else and swore. Not only was the game cancelled, but also a thief had stolen his new Porsche. On top of all this, everything was at a standstill because of the earthquake.

The car was missing for a few days, as the police were busy dealing with all the problems caused by the earthquake. At last they found the red Porsche. It was under the collapsed Nimitz freeway. And the thief was still in it. He had died trying to escape in the car he had snatched.

Although this story spread round the world very quickly in 1989, there was no truth in it. **F**

Harbor Terminals SECOND RIGHT

The thief in this myth picked the wrong day to steal a car.

DEATH BY RAT LOOK-ALIKE

There is an urban myth that rats come up from the sewers into people's houses. A man called Charles had a terrible fear of rats. He went into the bathroom where his wife had left her wig beside the toilet. The shock of believing that it was a huge rat gave him a heart attack. **T**

This really happened in France in 1988!

villain 'bad guy' in a story

BACK TO FRONT

A biker wore his jacket back-to-front to stop the cold getting through a gap in the zip. When he crashed and fell off his bike, a passer-by thought the crash had made the biker's head twist right round. He tried to turn the head back and broke the motorcyclist's neck. Ⓕ

Just a myth – but you should never move an injured motorcyclist. 🏍

None of these poor men deserved to come to a sticky end. Even so, it makes you wonder…

THE UNLUCKY HUSBAND

A man needed to climb on to his roof to adjust the television aerial, so he tied a rope round himself for extra safety. He fixed the other end of the rope to the bumper of his car on the other side of the house. But he did not tell his wife what he was doing before he climbed on to the roof. Mistake.

His wife needed to dash to the shops and decided to take the car. She drove off, pulled her husband from the roof and dragged him all the way there. Ⓕ

scuba diver   diver who uses breathing apparatus and oxygen

FRIED ON THE ICE

A man went ice fishing in Canada. He drove his jeep on to a frozen lake and let his dog out. The man found a place to cut a hole in the ice for his fishing line. The ice was so thick that he could not cut through and he decided to cheat. He got a stick of dynamite, lit the fuse and threw it across the ice. The dog barked and ran after it. The dog was well-trained so it picked up the dynamite and ran back to his master, who screamed before diving for cover in his jeep. This scared the dog, so it hid... under the jeep. Booom!

All dog lovers will be pleased this is false. Ⓕ

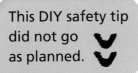

This DIY safety tip did not go as planned.

POACHED IN A WET SUIT

After a forest fire, a dead **scuba diver** was found in the ashes. He had not died from burns but from a fall. It seems he had come from the sea. Fire fighters had used helicopters to scoop up sea water to drop on the fire. They had scooped up the diver too. Ⓕ

SHRINK-WRAP

In the 1970s, it was the **craze** to wear jeans very tight. A girl bought the latest shrink-to-fit jeans for a perfect skin-tight fit. She squeezed them on then sat in the bath so they would soak and shrink. It was the crushing force of the jeans that killed her. Ⓕ

This could only happen in an urban myth. ≫

DON'T TRY THIS AT HOME

Police often come across mysterious deaths and have to work out what happened. When a dead body is found in a house, it could be the start of yet another urban myth…

KITCHEN MYSTERY

A 39-year-old man **crammed** far too many clothes into his top-loading washing machine. As they would not fit, he climbed on top of the washer to force the clothes inside. That was when he kicked the machine's 'on' button by mistake. The washing machine filled with water and began to turn. He lost his balance and both feet went down into the machine, where they got stuck.

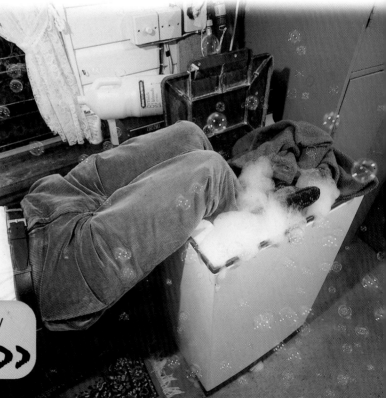

cram   to push too much into something

IN A SPIN

As the machine started its super-wash cycle, the man began thrashing around. Suddenly the machine stopped. His head banged against a shelf, knocking over a bottle of bleach. It poured over his face, blinding him and splashing in his mouth. At this point the washing machine flew into its high-speed spin cycle. He spun at 110 kilometres (70 miles) per hour. His head smashed against a steel beam behind the washing machine, killing him outright.

The police thought a killer had poisoned the man with bleach, bashed him on the head and then tried to hide the body in the washing machine. They arrested his wife for murder! ●

A Toronto skyscraper is the scene of this modern myth.

CANADA IN THE FALL

A lawyer in a Toronto skyscraper was showing some students how tough his office windows were. He pushed against the glass with his shoulder to show its strength but he crashed through the window. He plunged 24 floors to his death on the street below. Ⓣ

craze   passing fad or fashion

43

CLASSIC MIXTURE

POP ROCKS

Pop rocks were sweets that popped and fizzed in the mouth. They were taken off the market in the 1980s after a court case. A boy ate six bags of pop rocks washed down by fizzy cola. His stomach exploded.

A great story, but you can still buy pop rocks and they are safe! Ⓕ

Perhaps more than just your teeth are at risk if you mix candy and cola! **»**

Urban myths about food are some of the old favourites. When we got a taste for fast food we also got a taste for telling tales about it...

RODENT TAKE-AWAY

A young couple went to the local takeaway and bought fried chicken with fries. When they got home they turned off the lights, switched on the television and began to eat. They had nearly finished when they both agreed the chicken had an unusual taste. They turned on the light to look more closely. It looked like there was a piece of string on the plate. But it was a tail. The chicken had really been a fried rat!

Things like this may sometimes happen. ⓘ

dissolve　mix completely and evenly
version　another form of the same story

NICE!

On 28 November 2000, a woman called Katherine bought a box of deep-fried chicken wings in Virginia, USA. When she got them home, she put them out on plates for her family.

Katherine looked again at one of the chicken pieces. It was not like the others. It had an odd shape. She turned it round and then threw it down on the table. It was a chicken's head. It was deep fried, complete with eyes and a beak.

This is probably based on a true story but there are many **versions** of it. Most people seem to know someone who bought a chicken takeaway and got more than they wanted. Ⓣ ❓

COLA MYTHS

- It became fizzy by accident when a factory worker dropped soda into a vat.
- If you leave a tooth in cola overnight it will totally **dissolve**.
- Only two people at Coca-Cola know the secret **formula**. They only know half each in case one is kidnapped.

All of these rumours are Ⓕ

Some restaurants do not like to waste anything... ❮❮

formula   chemical symbols showing how something is made

CACTUS TALES

You cannot beat good stories about plants that fight back. And they could be true.

DESERTED IN THE DESERT

In the Arizona desert in the USA there are huge cacti as big as trees. Some are hundreds of years old and they are protected by law. But one cowboy did not bother about the law. He was out with his shotgun and he wanted to shoot at cacti. He stood close to a giant old cactus and blasted a few holes in its trunk. A great branch gave way and fell right on top of him. It crushed him flat and stabbed him with hundreds of spikes. Alone and unable to crawl away, he died from his wounds. (T)

DID YOU KNOW?

One type of cactus is home to a beetle that is put in your strawberry milkshake. Red food colouring is made from ground-up South American beetles. It is called cochineal and carmine.

Just another gross myth? Sorry – this one is really true! (T)

These cochineal beetles really are added to the food you eat!

This cactus fought back.

Why are peole
so scared of
tarantulas? ‹‹

THE TRUTH ABOUT TARANTULAS

There must be more urban myths about tarantulas than any other spider. People believe that tarantulas are violent and have a deadly bite. Ⓕ

They are actually quite shy and do not attack unless **provoked**. Bites usually cause little harm to humans.

TAKE COVER

A woman always brought back something new for her house when she went away. On one holiday to a very hot country, she brought back a large rare cactus in a huge pot. It looked great in her hallway so she asked some friends around to show them.

During her friends' visit there was a storm and the lights went off.

Candles and torches came out. Suddenly someone screamed, 'Look! The cactus is moving. It's alive!'

Everyone ran out and called the police. A cactus expert came to take a close look. Hundreds of deadly baby spiders were crawling from the cactus, on the march for food. Ⓕ

YOU CAN'T BEAT A GOOD TUNE

A music student had to write a tune for his **coursework**. He went to the library and found something written by his **professor**. He copied it out backwards, note for note and gave it in. It came back with the comment, 'This is "I'm Dreaming of a White Christmas".'

Even this teacher had cheated in the past.

CLASSIC MUSIC

Some urban myths are clearly pure **fiction**. We still like to believe they could happen. Some of the funny ones are set in public places where people are supposed to behave properly. But the fun starts when something goes very wrong.

THE MAD TROMBONIST

An orchestra was playing a piece of classical music that had guns firing at the end. A trombonist lit a firework and put it down his trombone to make the concert more exciting. He wanted to make a sound like a canon going off.

conductor   the person in front of an orchestra who controls the music

The firework shot out from the front of the trombone. It flew into the **conductor**, throwing him backwards off the stage.

GRAND FINALE

The conductor fell on to the front row of the audience. The chairs knocked into the seats behind. Seats fell backwards row-by-row as the audience went down like a row of dominoes. Legs waved in the air as people fell backwards. Meanwhile, a jet of hot gas shot through the trombone's mouthpiece and slammed into the trombonist's face. The bang burned his lips and knocked him out.

Later, from his hospital bed, he said through his bandages, 'I thought the end of my trombone would shield me from the explosion. I wanted the concert to end with a bang.' It did that all right.

A concert that went off with a bang.

FRONT TO BACK

John Lennon wrote a song called 'Because'. It was on the Beatle's album *Abbey Road*. But people said if they played it backwards it was another tune. It turned into a well-known piano piece by Beethoven, *The Moonlight Sonata*.

It is not quite the same.

FAULTY GOODS

People often say:

- Out of every 100 parachutes, the factory gets three twisted.
- Cars built on Friday afternoons have a 90 per cent chance of having faulty brakes.
- Some cheap frozen dinners have human fingernails inside.

They are just more classic myths! ⓕ

TRUE CLASSIC – THAT IS FALSE!

There are thousands of urban myths going around all the time. They are always changing and turning up with new twists. No collection of urban myths would be complete without this famous horror story. Everyone knows it is false, but we still like to feel an icy shiver when we hear it told. This is one **version**.

THE HOOK

A young couple sat in a car in Lovers Lane. The girl was **nervous** after the radio reported that a mad killer was on the loose. He was called 'The Hook' because one of his hands was missing and he wore a hook in its place.

Parachutists hope these urban myths are false. ≫

JUST IN TIME

The girl would not stop talking about 'The Hook' with his hood and the deadly weapon on the end of his arm. The boy got fed up and decided to drive her home. He lost his temper and drove off really fast. He did not say a word on the way home. When they arrived at the girl's house, he got out of the car and went round to open her door. On the door, there was a hook hanging from the handle.

This story may be false, but it is based on real events – like the Lovers Lane murders that happened in Texarkana, Texas, in the USA in 1946.

THE SCORE

From about 75 urban myths in this book, this chart shows how the score stands:

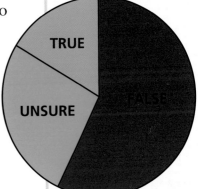

TRUE

UNSURE

FALSE

It may not tell us a lot about urban myths other than *you can never really be sure.*

'The Hook' has all the ingredients of a great urban myth. It is scary. It has a great twist. And it could happen to anyone...

51

FIND OUT MORE

WEBSITES

AMERICAN FOLKLORE

Includes myths, tall tales and ghost stories from across the USA.
americanfolklore.net

SPIDER MYTHS

Myths about all types of arachnids.
spiders.ucr.edu

BOOKS

Stranger Than Fiction: Urban Myths, Glanville Healey (Longman, 1999)

The Vanishing Hitchhiker: American Urban Legends and Their Meanings, Jan Harold Brunvand (W.W. Norton, 2003)

The Big Book of Urban Legends, Jan Harold Brundvan (Paradox Press, 2000)

WORLD WIDE WEB

If you want to find out more about **urban myths**, you can search the Internet using keywords like these:

- 'urban myths'
- urban + legends
- amazing stories

You can also find your own keywords by using headings or words from this book. The search tips opposite will help you find the most useful websites.

SEARCH TIPS

There are billions of pages on the Internet so it can be difficult to find exactly what you are looking for. For example, if you just type in 'water' on a search engine like Google, you will get a list of 19 million web pages. These search skills will help you find useful websites more quickly:

- Know exactly what you want to find out about first
- Use simple keywords instead of whole sentences
- Use two to six keywords in a search, putting the most important words first
- Be precise – only use names of people, places or things
- If you want to find words that go together, put quote marks around them, for example 'urban myth' or 'tarantula myths'
- Use the advanced section of your search engine.

WHERE TO LOOK

SEARCH ENGINE

A search engine looks through the entire web and lists all the sites that match the keywords. It can give thousands of links, but the best matches are at the top of the list. Try searching with **bbc.co.uk/search**

SEARCH DIRECTORY

A search directory is more like a library of websites. You can search by keyword or subject and browse through the different sites like you would look through books on a library shelf. A good example is **yahooligans.com**

GLOSSARY

A&E accident and emergency department in a hospital

absurd crazy or ridiculous

ambush to lie in wait to attack

awkward shy and foolish

bizarre very strange or weird

cashier person who works on a till or at a bank

cleaver knife with a heavy, wide blade

conductor person in front of an orchestra who controls the music

coursework projects completed during a course of study

cram to push too much into something

craze passing fad or fashion

culprit guilty person

defrost to remove frost

dissolve mix completely and evenly

disturb break someone's rest

embarrass to cause to feel **awkward** and ashamed

fake something that looks real but is not

far-fetched unconvincing

fiction made-up story from the imagination

formula chemical symbols showing how something is made

gap year break between school and further education

grisly causing horror and disgust

hoax joke, trick or something that is not real

intruder burglar who breaks in to someone's property

last respects final farewell to someone who has died

last rites final prayers for someone about to die

leathers clothes for wearing on a motorcycle

legend story based on a grain of truth

lie detector machine that records a person's reactions during questioning

lurk to wait around, ready to strike

myth made-up tale, told over the years and handed on

nervous easily scared

outback Australia's wild country, miles from the towns

pacemaker electronic device for helping to steady the heart beat

paddy field flooded field where rice is grown

Pekinese breed of small dog with long hair and a snub nose

professor teacher in a university

provoke to annoy or to stir into action

rambling lots of parts all over the place

remote far-away place in the middle of nowhere

reptiles group of cold-blooded creatures like snakes, lizards and crocodiles

rumour story based on gossip

scuba diver diver who uses breathing apparatus and oxygen

scrub thorny bushes and tufts of grass

sinister harmful or evil

suction gripping from removal of air and causing a vacuum

surgical spirit flammable fluid used for keeping things clean

tall story tale that is very silly and hard to believe

talons claws of a bird of prey

technology use of machines and equipment for doing tasks

thrive to grow with strength and health

trade buying and selling goods

undertaker someone who arranges funerals

urban myth a modern popular story that could be true but probably is not

version another form of the same story

villain 'bad guy' in a story

INDEX